welcome to your editorial planner for the next year

COPYRIGHT AND PERMISSIONS

EPICBLOG
ONE-YEAR EDITORIAL PLANNER

. . . .

. . . .

Permissions

Please feel free to take photos of this planner (or your use of it) for the purposes of review or social media sharing. Please do not photograph the whole planner.

. . . .

TABLE OF CONTENTS

ORIENTATION TO YOUR EDITORIAL PLANNER

WELCOME, CREATIVE GENIUS

LET A PENCIL BE YOUR BEST FRIEND AS YOU USE THIS PLANNER. MAINLY BECAUSE YOU'RE A CREATIVE GENIUS . . . AND AS YOU MAY KNOW, THINGS CHANGE––IT'S BEST TO BE ABLE TO ERASE THOSE THINGS.

THIS IS NOT A TRADITIONAL MONTHLY PLANNER. THIS IS AN EDITORIAL PLANNER THAT HELPS YOU BRAINSTORM, ORGANIZE, AND CREATE COMPELLING CONTENT AND PRODUCTS FOR YOUR BLOG (FOR 12 MONTHS, BUT YOU CAN START USING IT IN ANY MONTH).

THE PROCESS

ONE ON PAGES 6 - 23, CREATE A MINI BUSINESS PLAN FOR YOUR BLOG, RECORD YOUR PURPOSES AND PROCESSES, AND GET AN IDEA OF WHAT YOU WANT TO ACCOMPLISH THIS YEAR THROUGH YOUR BLOG.

TWO USE PAGES 102 - 113 THROUGHOUT THE YEAR AS A PLACE TO KEEP A RUNNING LIST OF ALL YOUR BLOG POST SERIES IDEAS, BLOG THEME IDEAS, PRODUCT IDEAS, COLLABORATION AND SPONSORED POST IDEAS, AS WELL AS JUST BLOG POST IDEAS IN GENERAL. THIS WILL KEEP YOU FOCUSED THROUGHOUT THE YEAR AND HELP YOU NOT FORGET ANY BLOG IDEAS THAT COME TO YOU. IF YOU'RE EVER SITTING AROUND LOOKING FOR SOMETHING TO DO, YOUR LISTS WILL HELP.

THREE DO YOUR MONTHLY THEME PLANNING FOR THE YEAR ON PAGES 28 + 29, BY FILLING OUT THE NAME OF EACH MONTH, THE THEME, AND ANY NOTES OR CONTENT IDEAS.

EVEN IF YOU CHANGE YOUR MIND ABOUT YOUR THEMES LATER, IT HELPS TO BRAINSTORM AND HAVE AN OVERALL PICTURE OF WHERE YOUR BLOG IS GOING.

ORIENTATION TO YOUR EDITORIAL PLANNER

FOUR IN THE MONTHLY PLANNING SECTION (EXAMPLE ON PAGE 32), RECORD THE MONTH NAME + THEME, THEN YOUR BLOG POST IDEAS, EMAIL LIST IDEAS, PRODUCT IDEAS, AND MORE, SO YOU CAN HAVE AN OVERVIEW OF ALL THE CONTENT YOU WANT TO RELEASE OR PROMOTE EACH MONTH.

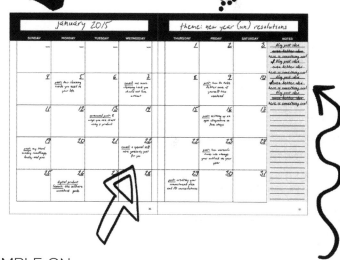

FIVE IN THE MONTHLY CALENDAR SECTION (STARTING ON PAGE 30), WRITE DOWN YOUR EDITORIAL THEME, THEN PLACE YOUR CONTENT IDEAS AND OTHER EVENTS, NEEDS, OR TASKS ON THEIR PLANNED DATES.

YOU CAN USE THE SIDEBAR TO WRITE NOTES OR KEEP A LIST OF ALL THE BLOG POSTS YOU PLAN TO ADD THAT MONTH.

SIX IN THE MONTHLY TRACKING SECTION (EXAMPLE ON PAGE 34), RECORD YOUR "BEGINNING OF MONTH GOALS" AND "END OF MONTH REVIEW" ON THE TWO PAGES FOLLOWING EACH MONTH'S CALENDAR AND CONTENT PLANS.

SEVEN REVIEW AND ADJUST THE PLANS + CONTENT IN YOUR EDITORIAL WORKBOOK FREQUENTLY THROUGHOUT THE YEAR. THIS IS THE SIMPLEST WAY I (byRegina.com) HAVE FOUND TO KEEP A FOCUSED, CONSISTENT, PROFITABLE BLOG PRESENCE GOING. I HOPE YOU ENJOY, MY FRIEND.

What are three things your blog will stand for this year?

1.

2.

3.

What are three promises you're making to your blog community this year?

1.

2.

3.

and now, a mini business plan for your blog

WELCOME TO YOUR MINI BUSINESS PLAN

At the very least, it's good to create or modify your business plan once per year. In reality, it should be an ever-changing document that helps guide you through decisions and keeps you on track with your blog.

. . . .

Fill out the next few pages (or create a document in your computer) with the requested information and prompts. Consider revisiting your plan once per month as you create your editorial calendars and content (starting on page 26 of this planner).

Having your business plan and your planner in the same place will help you form content and strategies that meet your goals + objectives. It's a great way to narrow down which pieces of content you should develop and which ones you should replace with something more fitting for your needs.

. . . .

If you want to do a longer business plan for your blog, visit byRegina.com/blog-business-plan.

Vision Statement
Write a short paragraph that explains why your blog exists, where you see it going in the future, and how you want readers/society to view your blog.

Mission Statement
Write a sentence or two that explains your responsibilities to your audience/community and how you'll accomplish your vision (above) in a practical way.

Culture Statement
Write a few sentences or bullet points on the type of "culture" your blog will create or embody. Everything from tone and appearance to personality and customs.

Blog Objectives

Write 3 - 5 measurable objectives for your blog in the next 6 to 12 months. Use actual numbers and goal dates so you'll be able to track your progress toward these goals.

Keys to Success

Now that you have some solid objectives in mind, figure out some corresponding keys to success. In other words: what absolutely needs to happen for you to reach your goals?

Future Expansion Plans

Even though you will be working hard on your immediate goals above, it's important to recognize and record your future plans for continued greatness.

PLATFORM + REPUTATION GOALS

○ develop a platform to sell one-on-one coaching services

○ develop a platform for speaking engagements

○ develop a platform to teach workshops and/or online classes

○ develop a platform to write + sell books and eBooks

○ increase your blog's popularity and get more organic web traffic that purchases products through affiliate links or helps you make advertising revenue

○ build a community around your brand

○ make money by selling low- to medium-cost products/systems to your clients

○ make money by selling high-cost & quality products/systems

○ attract new customers who've never bought similar items

○ attract new customers away from competitors

○ establish your expertise in your field and be a recognized name in your industry or among your target clients

○ _____

○ _____

○ _____

○ _____

○ _____

○ _____

○ _____

BLOG MONETIZATION METHODS

- ○ pay per click (PPC) ad networks
- ○ pay per view (PPV) ad networks
- ○ custom web advertisement space
- ○ product-specific affiliate programs
- ○ general affiliate/associate ad programs
- ○ selling services
- ○ selling digital products
- ○ selling physical products
- ○ creating a membership site or program
- ○ giving exclusive access to special content for a fee
- ○ creating sponsored posts
- ○ _____
- ○ _____
- ○ _____
- ○ _____
- ○ _____
- ○ _____
- ○ _____
- ○ _____
- ○ _____
- ○ _____
- ○ _____
- ○ _____
- ○ _____
- ○ _____
- ○ _____

Visit byRegina.com/make-money-blogging/ for blog monetization ideas + explanations.

Freelance or Consulting Services

Even if you don't pursue them immediately, record any ideas for current or future service offerings.

Physical and Digital Products

Write down any ideas you have for physical + digital products.

Other Monetization Methods

Any other unique ideas you want to record?

Reader Acquisition Strategy

Write a short paragraph (or bullet points) that detail how you intend to attract new readers to your blog this year.

Reader Retention + Community Creation Strategy

Write a sentence or two on how you plan to retain the readers who come your way. What will make them stay on your blog in the moment and return in the future? How will you build community around your blog?

Social Media Strategy

Write a paragraph or two that explains how you will use social media to grow your brand. Feel free to extend your statements in digital form--make a plan for each platform you'll be using.

Online (non-SM) Promotion Strategy

Record some of the things you will do online to promote your blog that are not social media (things such as: email, SEO, guest blogging, collaborations, commenting on other blogs, blog directories, etc.).

Offline Promotion + Growth Strategy

What organizations and opportunities exist IRL (in real life) for you to take part in to grow your brand's reach? Think of workshops, meetups, community groups, or classes you can teach or attend.

Identify at least 3 – 5 blogs in each category below to follow and use for inspiration + research purposes.

Brother Blogs
Find blogs that have similar focuses and audience sizes to keep track of. You'll often find these blog owners are great for collaborations or guest posts.

Aunt Blogs
Find blogs in the same niche that are at an audience/income size you'd like to reach in the future. Keep track of what they do that works and what they do that you'd improve on.

Cousin Blogs
Find blogs in another niche that you enjoy. Read them for inspiration and any ideas that you can carry over in your own way to your own industry.

Learnin' Blogs
Identify a few blogs from which you can learn more about your craft and more about blogging/business.

and now,
a bit about
your ideal
readers

Basic Demographics

Gender:

Age:

Location:

Ethnicity:

Education level:

Income level:

Industry/job:

Household composition and marital status:

Religious preferences:

Political preferences:

Preferences

Interests:

Hobbies:

Passions:

Personality:

Types of blogs he/she is likely to read:

Which magazines does he/she read?

What would make her/him trust a new source/blog/brand?

Which social issues are likely to affect her/him?

Is your ideal reader satisfied with her/his job? [Y/N] Why or why not?

What is her/his primary need or concern in life?

What's her/his general disposition? How does he/she view the world?

Some Favorites + Habits

Favorite book:

Favorite type of restaurant/food:

Favorite type of movie:

If he/she had a completely free day, what would they spend it doing?

Does he/she enjoy traveling? Where is he/she most likely to go in the next year?

What type of computer does he/she use? What type of device will they likely first access your brand on?

How is he/she most likely to first hear about a blog like yours (and/or services + products such as yours)?

Who else influences her/his buying decisions for a service or product such as what you offer?

How long would he/she typically take to decide on purchasing from you (if you sell from your blog)?

What's her/his general opinion of people in your profession?

What will make her/him trust and respect someone in your profession/niche?

List five questions he/she is most likely to have about you, your blog topic, or your products:

List the top three reasons he/she might "follow" you online or read your content regularly:

Social + Online Habits

Does he/she use these networks? If so, how often? What does he/she use them for?

Pinterest:

Facebook:

Instagram:

Twitter:

Google+:

YouTube:

LinkedIn:

Other social networks:

Email:

Does he/she have a smartphone? [Y/N] On which network(s), email platform, and device is he/she most likely to share information or recommendations with their friends?

What would make her/him share your blog or products with others?

Ideal Reader Brief

Write a summary, in your own words, of your ideal reader. Name her, crack a joke he would like, or simply write down a short description of the person that will remind you of them before you write (or tackle a product project).

and now, for your blog post process and style

Record your steps for creating a stellar blog post below. Refer back to this checklist each time you create a post. Include steps for editing and promoting your post as well.

○

○

○

○

○

○

○

○

○

○

○

○

○

○

○

○

○

○

○

On the next few pages, sketch out your ideal image style for all the different categories of posts you will create.

BLOG POST CATEGORIES

Write down the main categories in which you will add blog posts.

_____

_____

_____

_____

_____

_____

_____

_____

_____

_____

_____

_____

_____

THE THINGS THAT SCARE

YOU ARE THE THINGS

you'll build

your legacy on

HOW TO USE THE MONTHLY THEME PAGES

1. Fill out the months of the year for the next 12 months. Because they are blank, you can start using these pages in any month.

2. Fill out your ideal theme (or goal/series) for the month. Perhaps use a pencil in case you change your mind.

MONTH	*january*	THEME	*new year (un) resolutions*
CONTENT IDEAS			

MONTH	*february*	THEME	
CONTENT IDEAS			

MONTH	*march*	THEME	
CONTENT IDEAS			

MONTH	*april*	THEME	
CONTENT IDEAS			

MONTH	*may*	THEME	
CONTENT IDEAS			

MONTH	*june*	THEME	*intentional living and intentional business*
CONTENT IDEAS	*6 ways to live more intentionally, something with the intentional living affiliate class, how to build your values into your business without offending others, the intentional business workbook, something with a free download*		

MONTH	*july*	THEME	*get your life in summer shape*
CONTENT IDEAS			

MONTH	*august*	THEME	
CONTENT IDEAS			

MONTH	*september*	THEME	
CONTENT IDEAS			

MONTH	*october*	THEME	
CONTENT IDEAS			

MONTH	*november*	THEME	
CONTENT IDEAS			

MONTH	*december*	THEME	
CONTENT IDEAS			

3. Now, fill out content ideas, notes, blog post titles, sponsored post ideas, or giveaways + collaborations, etc. Don't forget you'll have even more room on each month's individual calendar.

and

for your theme, and income

now,

monthly goal, planning

MONTH   **THEME**

CONTENT IDEAS

MONTH   **THEME**

CONTENT IDEAS

MONTH   **THEME**

CONTENT IDEAS

MONTH   **THEME**

CONTENT IDEAS

MONTH   **THEME**

CONTENT IDEAS

MONTH   **THEME**

CONTENT IDEAS

MONTH   **THEME**

CONTENT IDEAS

MONTH   **THEME**

CONTENT IDEAS

MONTH   **THEME**

CONTENT IDEAS

MONTH   **THEME**

CONTENT IDEAS

MONTH   **THEME**

CONTENT IDEAS

MONTH   **THEME**

CONTENT IDEAS

SUNDAY	MONDAY	TUESDAY	WEDNESDAY
—	—	—	—
—	—	—	—
—	—	—	—
—	—	—	—
—	—	—	—

THURSDAY	FRIDAY	SATURDAY	NOTES
—	—	—	
—	—	—	
—	—	—	
—	—	—	
—	—	—	

DATE/ORDER	TOPIC/TITLE	IMAGES/SUPPLIES

EMAIL LIST CONTENT

PRODUCT IDEAS

**COLLABORATIONS OR
SPONSORED CONTENT**

MONTH: _____ THEME: _____

HOW MANY BLOG POSTS DO YOU WANT TO ADD TO YOUR SITE THIS MONTH?

WHAT WILL YOU DO THIS MONTH TO CONTINUE TO BUILD COMMUNITY OR ENCOURAGE BLOG GROWTH?

WHAT IS YOUR EMAIL STRATEGY THIS MONTH? WHAT WILL YOU BE EMAILING OUT TO YOUR SUBSCRIBERS?

WHAT ARE THE THREE MOST IMPORTANT THINGS FOR YOU TO ACCOMPLISH THIS MONTH? HOW WILL YOU FEEL ONCE THEY'RE DONE?

BLOG MAINTENANCE TASKS	PRODUCT CREATION OR PROJECT TASKS
○	○
○	○
○	○
○	○
○	○
○	○
○	○
○	○
○	○
○	○
○	○
○	○

STATS	LAST MONTH	THIS MONTH	CHANGE (+/-)
# OF BLOG POSTS ADDED			
BLOG VISITORS			
PAGEVIEWS			
EMAIL SUBSCRIBERS			
5 MOST POPULAR POSTS			
5 MOST POPULAR TRAFFIC SOURCES			
BOUNCE RATE			
AVERAGE SESSION TIME			
MOST POPULAR PRODUCT			
TOTAL INCOME			
TOTAL EXPENSES			

BLOG INCOME

○
○
○
○
○
○
○
○
○
○
○
○

BLOG EXPENSES

○
○
○
○
○
○
○
○
○
○
○
○

SUNDAY	MONDAY	TUESDAY	WEDNESDAY
—	—	—	—
—	—	—	—
—	—	—	—
—	—	—	—
—	—	—	—

THURSDAY	FRIDAY	SATURDAY	NOTES
—	—	—	
—	—	—	
—	—	—	
—	—	—	
—	—	—	

DATE/ORDER	TOPIC/TITLE	IMAGES/SUPPLIES

EMAIL LIST CONTENT

PRODUCT IDEAS

**COLLABORATIONS OR
SPONSORED CONTENT**

MONTH: _____ THEME: _____

HOW MANY BLOG POSTS DO YOU WANT TO ADD TO YOUR SITE THIS MONTH?

WHAT WILL YOU DO THIS MONTH TO CONTINUE TO BUILD COMMUNITY OR ENCOURAGE BLOG GROWTH?

WHAT IS YOUR EMAIL STRATEGY THIS MONTH? WHAT WILL YOU BE EMAILING OUT TO YOUR SUBSCRIBERS?

WHAT ARE THE THREE MOST IMPORTANT THINGS FOR YOU TO ACCOMPLISH THIS MONTH? HOW WILL YOU FEEL ONCE THEY'RE DONE?

BLOG MAINTENANCE TASKS	PRODUCT CREATION OR PROJECT TASKS
○	○
○	○
○	○
○	○
○	○
○	○
○	○
○	○
○	○
○	○
○	○
○	○

STATS	LAST MONTH	THIS MONTH	CHANGE (+/-)
# OF BLOG POSTS ADDED			
BLOG VISITORS			
PAGEVIEWS			
EMAIL SUBSCRIBERS			
5 MOST POPULAR POSTS			
5 MOST POPULAR TRAFFIC SOURCES			
BOUNCE RATE			
AVERAGE SESSION TIME			
MOST POPULAR PRODUCT			
TOTAL INCOME			
TOTAL EXPENSES			

BLOG INCOME	BLOG EXPENSES
○	○
○	○
○	○
○	○
○	○
○	○
○	○
○	○
○	○
○	○
○	○
○	○

SUNDAY	MONDAY	TUESDAY	WEDNESDAY
—	—	—	—
—	—	—	—
—	—	—	—
—	—	—	—
—	—	—	—

THURSDAY	FRIDAY	SATURDAY	NOTES
—	—	—	
—	—	—	
—	—	—	
—	—	—	
—	—	—	

DATE/ORDER	TOPIC/TITLE	IMAGES/SUPPLIES

EMAIL LIST CONTENT

PRODUCT IDEAS

COLLABORATIONS OR SPONSORED CONTENT

MONTH: _____ THEME: _____

HOW MANY BLOG POSTS DO YOU WANT TO ADD TO YOUR SITE THIS MONTH?

WHAT WILL YOU DO THIS MONTH TO CONTINUE TO BUILD COMMUNITY OR ENCOURAGE BLOG GROWTH?

WHAT IS YOUR EMAIL STRATEGY THIS MONTH? WHAT WILL YOU BE EMAILING OUT TO YOUR SUBSCRIBERS?

WHAT ARE THE THREE MOST IMPORTANT THINGS FOR YOU TO ACCOMPLISH THIS MONTH? HOW WILL YOU FEEL ONCE THEY'RE DONE?

BLOG MAINTENANCE TASKS	PRODUCT CREATION OR PROJECT TASKS
○	○
○	○
○	○
○	○
○	○
○	○
○	○
○	○
○	○
○	○
○	○
○	○

STATS	LAST MONTH	THIS MONTH	CHANGE (+/−)
# OF BLOG POSTS ADDED			
BLOG VISITORS			
PAGEVIEWS			
EMAIL SUBSCRIBERS			
5 MOST POPULAR POSTS			
5 MOST POPULAR TRAFFIC SOURCES			
BOUNCE RATE			
AVERAGE SESSION TIME			
MOST POPULAR PRODUCT			
TOTAL INCOME			
TOTAL EXPENSES			

BLOG INCOME

○
○
○
○
○
○
○
○
○
○
○
○
○

BLOG EXPENSES

○
○
○
○
○
○
○
○
○
○
○
○
○

SUNDAY	MONDAY	TUESDAY	WEDNESDAY
—	—	—	—
—	—	—	—
—	—	—	—
—	—	—	—
—	—	—	—

DATE/ORDER	TOPIC/TITLE	IMAGES/SUPPLIES

EMAIL LIST CONTENT

PRODUCT IDEAS

COLLABORATIONS OR SPONSORED CONTENT

MONTH: _____ THEME: _____

HOW MANY BLOG POSTS DO YOU WANT TO ADD TO YOUR SITE THIS MONTH?

WHAT WILL YOU DO THIS MONTH TO CONTINUE TO BUILD COMMUNITY OR ENCOURAGE BLOG GROWTH?

WHAT IS YOUR EMAIL STRATEGY THIS MONTH? WHAT WILL YOU BE EMAILING OUT TO YOUR SUBSCRIBERS?

WHAT ARE THE THREE MOST IMPORTANT THINGS FOR YOU TO ACCOMPLISH THIS MONTH? HOW WILL YOU FEEL ONCE THEY'RE DONE?

BLOG MAINTENANCE TASKS	PRODUCT CREATION OR PROJECT TASKS
○	○
○	○
○	○
○	○
○	○
○	○
○	○
○	○
○	○
○	○
○	○
○	○

STATS	LAST MONTH	THIS MONTH	CHANGE (+/−)
# OF BLOG POSTS ADDED			
BLOG VISITORS			
PAGEVIEWS			
EMAIL SUBSCRIBERS			
5 MOST POPULAR POSTS			
5 MOST POPULAR TRAFFIC SOURCES			
BOUNCE RATE			
AVERAGE SESSION TIME			
MOST POPULAR PRODUCT			
TOTAL INCOME			
TOTAL EXPENSES			

BLOG INCOME	BLOG EXPENSES
○	○
○	○
○	○
○	○
○	○
○	○
○	○
○	○
○	○
○	○
○	○
○	○
○	○

SUNDAY	MONDAY	TUESDAY	WEDNESDAY
—	—	—	—
—	—	—	—
—	—	—	—
—	—	—	—
—	—	—	—

DATE/ORDER	TOPIC/TITLE	IMAGES/SUPPLIES

EMAIL LIST CONTENT

PRODUCT IDEAS

COLLABORATIONS OR SPONSORED CONTENT

MONTH: _____ THEME: _____

HOW MANY BLOG POSTS DO YOU WANT TO ADD TO YOUR SITE THIS MONTH?

WHAT WILL YOU DO THIS MONTH TO CONTINUE TO BUILD COMMUNITY OR ENCOURAGE BLOG GROWTH?

WHAT IS YOUR EMAIL STRATEGY THIS MONTH? WHAT WILL YOU BE EMAILING OUT TO YOUR SUBSCRIBERS?

WHAT ARE THE THREE MOST IMPORTANT THINGS FOR YOU TO ACCOMPLISH THIS MONTH? HOW WILL YOU FEEL ONCE THEY'RE DONE?

BLOG MAINTENANCE TASKS	PRODUCT CREATION OR PROJECT TASKS
○	○
○	○
○	○
○	○
○	○
○	○
○	○
○	○
○	○
○	○
○	○
○	○

STATS	LAST MONTH	THIS MONTH	CHANGE (+/-)
# OF BLOG POSTS ADDED			
BLOG VISITORS			
PAGEVIEWS			
EMAIL SUBSCRIBERS			
5 MOST POPULAR POSTS			
5 MOST POPULAR TRAFFIC SOURCES			
BOUNCE RATE			
AVERAGE SESSION TIME			
MOST POPULAR PRODUCT			
TOTAL INCOME			
TOTAL EXPENSES			

BLOG INCOME

- ◯
- ◯
- ◯
- ◯
- ◯
- ◯
- ◯
- ◯
- ◯
- ◯
- ◯
- ◯
- ◯

BLOG EXPENSES

- ◯
- ◯
- ◯
- ◯
- ◯
- ◯
- ◯
- ◯
- ◯
- ◯
- ◯
- ◯
- ◯

SUNDAY	MONDAY	TUESDAY	WEDNESDAY
—	—	—	—
—	—	—	—
—	—	—	—
—	—	—	—
—	—	—	—

THURSDAY	FRIDAY	SATURDAY	NOTES
—	—	—	
—	—	—	
—	—	—	
—	—	—	
—	—	—	

DATE/ORDER	TOPIC/TITLE	IMAGES/SUPPLIES

EMAIL LIST CONTENT

PRODUCT IDEAS

COLLABORATIONS OR SPONSORED CONTENT

MONTH: _____ THEME: _____

HOW MANY BLOG POSTS DO YOU WANT TO ADD TO YOUR SITE THIS MONTH?

WHAT WILL YOU DO THIS MONTH TO CONTINUE TO BUILD COMMUNITY OR ENCOURAGE BLOG GROWTH?

WHAT IS YOUR EMAIL STRATEGY THIS MONTH? WHAT WILL YOU BE EMAILING OUT TO YOUR SUBSCRIBERS?

WHAT ARE THE THREE MOST IMPORTANT THINGS FOR YOU TO ACCOMPLISH THIS MONTH? HOW WILL YOU FEEL ONCE THEY'RE DONE?

BLOG MAINTENANCE TASKS	PRODUCT CREATION OR PROJECT TASKS
○	○
○	○
○	○
○	○
○	○
○	○
○	○
○	○
○	○
○	○
○	○
○	○

STATS	LAST MONTH	THIS MONTH	CHANGE (+/-)
# OF BLOG POSTS ADDED			
BLOG VISITORS			
PAGEVIEWS			
EMAIL SUBSCRIBERS			
5 MOST POPULAR POSTS			
5 MOST POPULAR TRAFFIC SOURCES			
BOUNCE RATE			
AVERAGE SESSION TIME			
MOST POPULAR PRODUCT			
TOTAL INCOME			
TOTAL EXPENSES			

BLOG INCOME

○
○
○
○
○
○
○
○
○
○
○
○

BLOG EXPENSES

○
○
○
○
○
○
○
○
○
○
○
○
○

SUNDAY	MONDAY	TUESDAY	WEDNESDAY
—	—	—	—
—	—	—	—
—	—	—	—
—	—	—	—
—	—	—	—

DATE/ORDER	TOPIC/TITLE	IMAGES/SUPPLIES

EMAIL LIST CONTENT

PRODUCT IDEAS

COLLABORATIONS OR SPONSORED CONTENT

MONTH: _____ THEME: _____

HOW MANY BLOG POSTS DO YOU WANT TO ADD TO YOUR SITE THIS MONTH?

WHAT WILL YOU DO THIS MONTH TO CONTINUE TO BUILD COMMUNITY OR ENCOURAGE BLOG GROWTH?

WHAT IS YOUR EMAIL STRATEGY THIS MONTH? WHAT WILL YOU BE EMAILING OUT TO YOUR SUBSCRIBERS?

WHAT ARE THE THREE MOST IMPORTANT THINGS FOR YOU TO ACCOMPLISH THIS MONTH? HOW WILL YOU FEEL ONCE THEY'RE DONE?

BLOG MAINTENANCE TASKS	PRODUCT CREATION OR PROJECT TASKS
○	○
○	○
○	○
○	○
○	○
○	○
○	○
○	○
○	○
○	○
○	○
○	○

STATS	LAST MONTH	THIS MONTH	CHANGE (+/-)
# OF BLOG POSTS ADDED			
BLOG VISITORS			
PAGEVIEWS			
EMAIL SUBSCRIBERS			
5 MOST POPULAR POSTS			
5 MOST POPULAR TRAFFIC SOURCES			
BOUNCE RATE			
AVERAGE SESSION TIME			
MOST POPULAR PRODUCT			
TOTAL INCOME			
TOTAL EXPENSES			

BLOG INCOME	BLOG EXPENSES

- ○
- ○
- ○
- ○
- ○
- ○
- ○
- ○
- ○
- ○
- ○
- ○
- ○
- ○
- ○

- ○
- ○
- ○
- ○
- ○
- ○
- ○
- ○
- ○
- ○
- ○
- ○
- ○

SUNDAY	MONDAY	TUESDAY	WEDNESDAY
—	—	—	—
—	—	—	—
—	—	—	—
—	—	—	—
—	—	—	—

THURSDAY	FRIDAY	SATURDAY	NOTES
—	—	—	
—	—	—	
—	—	—	
—	—	—	
—	—	—	

DATE/ORDER	TOPIC/TITLE	IMAGES/SUPPLIES

EMAIL LIST CONTENT

PRODUCT IDEAS

COLLABORATIONS OR
SPONSORED CONTENT

MONTH: _____ THEME: _____

HOW MANY BLOG POSTS DO YOU WANT TO ADD TO YOUR SITE THIS MONTH?

WHAT WILL YOU DO THIS MONTH TO CONTINUE TO BUILD COMMUNITY OR ENCOURAGE BLOG GROWTH?

WHAT IS YOUR EMAIL STRATEGY THIS MONTH? WHAT WILL YOU BE EMAILING OUT TO YOUR SUBSCRIBERS?

WHAT ARE THE THREE MOST IMPORTANT THINGS FOR YOU TO ACCOMPLISH THIS MONTH? HOW WILL YOU FEEL ONCE THEY'RE DONE?

BLOG MAINTENANCE TASKS	PRODUCT CREATION OR PROJECT TASKS
○	○
○	○
○	○
○	○
○	○
○	○
○	○
○	○
○	○
○	○
○	○
○	○

STATS	LAST MONTH	THIS MONTH	CHANGE (+/-)
# OF BLOG POSTS ADDED			
BLOG VISITORS			
PAGEVIEWS			
EMAIL SUBSCRIBERS			
5 MOST POPULAR POSTS			
5 MOST POPULAR TRAFFIC SOURCES			
BOUNCE RATE			
AVERAGE SESSION TIME			
MOST POPULAR PRODUCT			
TOTAL INCOME			
TOTAL EXPENSES			

BLOG INCOME	BLOG EXPENSES
○	○
○	○
○	○
○	○
○	○
○	○
○	○
○	○
○	○
○	○
○	○
○	○
○	○
○	

SUNDAY	MONDAY	TUESDAY	WEDNESDAY
—	—	—	—
—	—	—	—
—	—	—	—
—	—	—	—
—	—	—	—

DATE/ORDER	TOPIC/TITLE	IMAGES/SUPPLIES

EMAIL LIST CONTENT

PRODUCT IDEAS

**COLLABORATIONS OR
SPONSORED CONTENT**

MONTH: _____ THEME: _____

HOW MANY BLOG POSTS DO YOU WANT TO ADD TO YOUR SITE THIS MONTH?

WHAT WILL YOU DO THIS MONTH TO CONTINUE TO BUILD COMMUNITY OR ENCOURAGE BLOG GROWTH?

WHAT IS YOUR EMAIL STRATEGY THIS MONTH? WHAT WILL YOU BE EMAILING OUT TO YOUR SUBSCRIBERS?

WHAT ARE THE THREE MOST IMPORTANT THINGS FOR YOU TO ACCOMPLISH THIS MONTH? HOW WILL YOU FEEL ONCE THEY'RE DONE?

BLOG MAINTENANCE TASKS	PRODUCT CREATION OR PROJECT TASKS
○	○
○	○
○	○
○	○
○	○
○	○
○	○
○	○
○	○
○	○
○	○
○	○

STATS	LAST MONTH	THIS MONTH	CHANGE (+/-)
# OF BLOG POSTS ADDED			
BLOG VISITORS			
PAGEVIEWS			
EMAIL SUBSCRIBERS			
5 MOST POPULAR POSTS			
5 MOST POPULAR TRAFFIC SOURCES			
BOUNCE RATE			
AVERAGE SESSION TIME			
MOST POPULAR PRODUCT			
TOTAL INCOME			
TOTAL EXPENSES			

BLOG INCOME

BLOG EXPENSES

○
○
○
○
○
○
○
○
○
○
○
○
○

○
○
○
○
○
○
○
○
○
○
○
○
○

SUNDAY	MONDAY	TUESDAY	WEDNESDAY
—	—	—	—
—	—	—	—
—	—	—	—
—	—	—	—
—	—	—	—

THURSDAY	FRIDAY	SATURDAY	NOTES
—	—	—	
—	—	—	
—	—	—	
—	—	—	
—	—	—	

DATE/ORDER	TOPIC/TITLE	IMAGES/SUPPLIES

EMAIL LIST CONTENT

PRODUCT IDEAS

COLLABORATIONS OR SPONSORED CONTENT

MONTH: _____ THEME: _____

HOW MANY BLOG POSTS DO YOU WANT TO ADD TO YOUR SITE THIS MONTH?

WHAT WILL YOU DO THIS MONTH TO CONTINUE TO BUILD COMMUNITY OR ENCOURAGE BLOG GROWTH?

WHAT IS YOUR EMAIL STRATEGY THIS MONTH? WHAT WILL YOU BE EMAILING OUT TO YOUR SUBSCRIBERS?

WHAT ARE THE THREE MOST IMPORTANT THINGS FOR YOU TO ACCOMPLISH THIS MONTH? HOW WILL YOU FEEL ONCE THEY'RE DONE?

BLOG MAINTENANCE TASKS	PRODUCT CREATION OR PROJECT TASKS
○	○
○	○
○	○
○	○
○	○
○	○
○	○
○	○
○	○
○	○
○	○
○	○

STATS	LAST MONTH	THIS MONTH	CHANGE (+/-)
# OF BLOG POSTS ADDED			
BLOG VISITORS			
PAGEVIEWS			
EMAIL SUBSCRIBERS			
5 MOST POPULAR POSTS			
5 MOST POPULAR TRAFFIC SOURCES			
BOUNCE RATE			
AVERAGE SESSION TIME			
MOST POPULAR PRODUCT			
TOTAL INCOME			
TOTAL EXPENSES			

BLOG INCOME

BLOG EXPENSES

SUNDAY	MONDAY	TUESDAY	WEDNESDAY
—	—	—	—
—	—	—	—
—	—	—	—
—	—	—	—
—	—	—	—

THURSDAY	FRIDAY	SATURDAY	NOTES
—	—	—	
—	—	—	
—	—	—	
—	—	—	
—	—	—	

DATE/ORDER	TOPIC/TITLE	IMAGES/SUPPLIES

EMAIL LIST CONTENT

PRODUCT IDEAS

**COLLABORATIONS OR
SPONSORED CONTENT**

MONTH: _____ THEME: _____

HOW MANY BLOG POSTS DO YOU WANT TO ADD TO YOUR SITE THIS MONTH?

WHAT WILL YOU DO THIS MONTH TO CONTINUE TO BUILD COMMUNITY OR ENCOURAGE BLOG GROWTH?

WHAT IS YOUR EMAIL STRATEGY THIS MONTH? WHAT WILL YOU BE EMAILING OUT TO YOUR SUBSCRIBERS?

WHAT ARE THE THREE MOST IMPORTANT THINGS FOR YOU TO ACCOMPLISH THIS MONTH? HOW WILL YOU FEEL ONCE THEY'RE DONE?

BLOG MAINTENANCE TASKS	PRODUCT CREATION OR PROJECT TASKS
○	○
○	○
○	○
○	○
○	○
○	○
○	○
○	○
○	○
○	○
○	○
○	○

STATS	LAST MONTH	THIS MONTH	CHANGE (+/-)
# OF BLOG POSTS ADDED			
BLOG VISITORS			
PAGEVIEWS			
EMAIL SUBSCRIBERS			
5 MOST POPULAR POSTS			
5 MOST POPULAR TRAFFIC SOURCES			
BOUNCE RATE			
AVERAGE SESSION TIME			
MOST POPULAR PRODUCT			
TOTAL INCOME			
TOTAL EXPENSES			

BLOG INCOME

○
○
○
○
○
○
○
○
○
○
○
○
○

BLOG EXPENSES

○
○
○
○
○
○
○
○
○
○
○
○
○

SUNDAY	MONDAY	TUESDAY	WEDNESDAY
—	—	—	—
—	—	—	—
—	—	—	—
—	—	—	—
—	—	—	—

THURSDAY	FRIDAY	SATURDAY	NOTES
—	—	—	
—	—	—	
—	—	—	
—	—	—	
—	—	—	

DATE/ORDER	TOPIC/TITLE	IMAGES/SUPPLIES

EMAIL LIST CONTENT

PRODUCT IDEAS

COLLABORATIONS OR
SPONSORED CONTENT

MONTH: _____ THEME: _____

HOW MANY BLOG POSTS DO YOU WANT TO ADD TO YOUR SITE THIS MONTH?

WHAT WILL YOU DO THIS MONTH TO CONTINUE TO BUILD COMMUNITY OR ENCOURAGE BLOG GROWTH?

WHAT IS YOUR EMAIL STRATEGY THIS MONTH? WHAT WILL YOU BE EMAILING OUT TO YOUR SUBSCRIBERS?

WHAT ARE THE THREE MOST IMPORTANT THINGS FOR YOU TO ACCOMPLISH THIS MONTH? HOW WILL YOU FEEL ONCE THEY'RE DONE?

BLOG MAINTENANCE TASKS	PRODUCT CREATION OR PROJECT TASKS
○	○
○	○
○	○
○	○
○	○
○	○
○	○
○	○
○	○
○	○
○	○
○	○

STATS	LAST MONTH	THIS MONTH	CHANGE (+/−)
# OF BLOG POSTS ADDED			
BLOG VISITORS			
PAGEVIEWS			
EMAIL SUBSCRIBERS			
5 MOST POPULAR POSTS			
5 MOST POPULAR TRAFFIC SOURCES			
BOUNCE RATE			
AVERAGE SESSION TIME			
MOST POPULAR PRODUCT			
TOTAL INCOME			
TOTAL EXPENSES			

BLOG INCOME

○
○
○
○
○
○
○
○
○
○
○
○

BLOG EXPENSES

○
○
○
○
○
○
○
○
○
○
○
○
○

BLOG POST IDEAS

THIS YEAR'S BLOG ACCOMPLISHMENTS

MONTH	THEME	GRADE	VISITORS	PAGEVIEWS	INCOME	EXPENSES

AFFILIATE + BLOG LOGINS

ACCOUNT	LOGIN URL	USERNAME	PASSWORD OR HINT

THANK YOU KINDLY

. . . .

HOPE YOU ENJOYED USING

YOUR PLANNER THIS YEAR.

PLEASE LET ME KNOW HOW YOU LIKED IT

AND HOW IT CAN IMPROVE.

TWITTER // INSTAGRAM // PINTEREST >>> @byReginaTV

plus.google.com/+byRegina

byRegina.com

. . . .

44640589R00066

Made in the USA
San Bernardino, CA
19 January 2017